LIGHTNING
BOLT
BOOKS™

German Shepherds

Sarah Frank

Lerner Publications ◆ Minneapolis

Lerner Publications Company
A division of Lerner Publishing Group, Inc.
241 First Avenue North
Minneapolis, MN 55401 USA

For reading level and more information, look up this title at www.lernerbooks.com.

Library of Congress Cataloging-in-Publication Data

Names: Frank, Sarah, author.
Title: German shepherds / Sarah Frank.
Description: Minneapolis : Lerner Publications, [2019] | Series: Lightning bolt books. Who's a good dog? | Audience: Age 6-9. | Audience: Grade K to 3. | Includes bibliographical references and index.
Identifiers: LCCN 2018004401 | ISBN 9781541538580 (lb : alk. paper)
Subjects: LCSH: German shepherd dog—Juvenile literature.
Classification: LCC SF429.G37 F73 2019 | DDC 636.737—dc23

LC record available at https://lccn.loc.gov/2018004401

Manufactured in the United States of America
1-45041-35868-6/13/2018

Table of Contents

A True Friend

Smart, brave, and loyal. Would you like a friend like that? Then meet your new best friend. This friend is furry and has four feet!

Many people call a German shepherd their best friend. These dogs are big and lovable. They weigh from 50 to 90 pounds (23 to 41 kg).

There's a lot to love about a shepherd.

This shepherd is a color called sable.

Shepherds can be many colors. Some are black and tan. Others are all black. Still others are dark brown.

All shepherds make great pets. They are eager and alert. And they love spending time with their owners.

What a gentle giant!

The Shepherd Story

No two dogs are alike. But certain breeds have things in common. The American Kennel Club (AKC) groups breeds by things they have in common. Shepherds are in the herding group.

German farmers had lots of sheep to herd!

Herding dogs are pros at herding. Long ago, most shepherds herded sheep in Germany.

These days, shepherds can be found around the world. They might herd sheep or goats. Or they might just be a family's favorite pet!

Not all herding dogs herd.

Many owners love how easy shepherds are to train.

All herding dogs are smart. They can easily learn tricks. What tricks would you like to teach a shepherd?

A Good Fit?

Shepherds are wonderful. But they aren't for everyone. A parent can help you decide if a shepherd is right for you.

Training any dog takes patience.

Shepherds are big and strong. They must be well trained. An untrained shepherd can be trouble. Does your family have time to train one?

Shepherds love to be with their people. They don't like being left alone. If you're away from home a lot, a shepherd isn't a good fit.

Lonely shepherds can get into things they aren't supposed to.

Shepherds need lots of exercise. A walk around the block isn't enough. They need long runs and nature hikes. If you're not into exercise, pass on a shepherd.

Shepherd Care

Maybe you've decided that a shepherd is perfect for you. If so, get ready to buy some dog supplies! A collar, doggy bowls, and toys are a good start.

Your dog will need to see a vet. The vet will check for any health problems. Vets also give pets the shots they need.

Help keep your pet healthy by giving it good food. The vet can help you choose a food. And don't give your shepherd table scraps. People food isn't good for dogs!

Dog food is the best thing to feed your shepherd.

Take good care of your shepherd. Your pooch will reward you. A happy, healthy shepherd will bring you lots of joy.

Doggone Good Tips!

- What's the perfect name for a shepherd? Here are some ideas: Baron, Heidi, Greta, Sarge, Ranger, Glory, or Rex.

- Take your shepherd on family outings. A well-trained shepherd can fit in at parks, picnics, or almost anywhere!

- Having a shepherd means vacuuming—a lot. These pooches tend to shed. But shepherd owners think it's a small price to pay for all the happiness they get from their dog.

Why Shepherds Are the Best

- Some are heroes! Shepherds have woken up their owners to warn them of a fire. They have pulled people from car accidents. They have scared off robbers by barking loudly.

- Shepherds also helped German soldiers in World War I (1914–1918). They stood guard at night. They tracked enemy soldiers. Their brains and bravery helped them do these jobs.

- Shepherds make great police dogs. Police can train the dogs to sniff out bombs or chase down bad guys. Police officers who work with shepherds praise their strength and loyalty.

Glossary

American Kennel Club (AKC): an organization that groups dogs by breed

breed: a particular type of dog. Dogs of the same breed have the same body shape and general features.

eager: very excited and interested

herding group: a group of dogs that have a natural ability to control the movement of other animals

loyal: having or showing support for someone

vet: a doctor who treats animals

Further Reading

American Kennel Club
http://www.akc.org

American Society for the Prevention of Cruelty to Animals
https://www.aspca.org

Boothroyd, Jennifer. *Hero Law Enforcement Dogs.* Minneapolis: Lerner Publications, 2017.

Gray, Susan H. *German Shepherds.* New York: AV2 by Weigl, 2017.

Mathea, Heidi. *German Shepherds.* Edina, MN: Abdo, 2011.

Index

Photo Acknowledgments

Image credits: TCGraphicDesign/Shutterstock.com, pp. 2, 6; Jagodka/Shutterstock.com, pp. 4, 23; Irina_Gulyaeva/Shutterstock.com, p. 5; Katarzyna Mazurowska/Shutterstock.com, p. 7; ChameleonsEye/Shutterstock.com, p. 8; Binder Medienagentur/Shutterstock.com, p. 9; Rohit Seth/Shutterstock.com, p. 10; Versta/Shutterstock.com, p. 11; Grigorita Ko/Shutterstock.com, p. 12; marcin jucha/Shutterstock.com, p. 13; Michelle D. Milliman/Shutterstock.com, p. 14; Adrian Vaju Photography/Shutterstock.com, p. 15; FabrikaSimf/Shutterstock.com, p. 16; ARLOU_ANDREI/Shutterstock.com, p. 17; Monika Wisniewska/Shutterstock.com, p. 18; Stone36/Shutterstock.com, p. 19.

Cover image: Eric Isselee/Shutterstock.com.

Main body text set in Billy Infant regular 28/36. Typeface provided by SparkType.